Birds of Denali
AN INTRODUCTION TO SELECTED SPECIES

Carol McIntyre, Nan Eagleson and Alan Seegert

Illustrations by David Allen Sibley

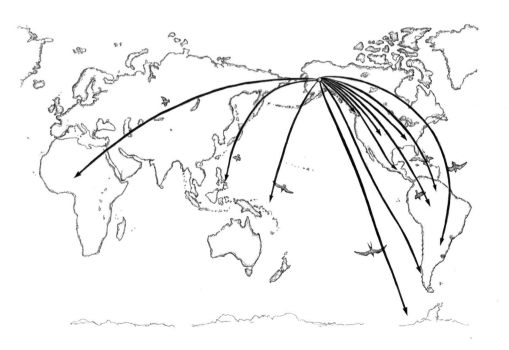

Alaska Natural History Association
SHARING ALASKA'S NATURAL AND CULTURAL HERITAGE

ACKNOWLEDGMENTS
The authors would like to acknowledge Anna Marie Bensen, Fred Dean, Debbie Nigro, Bob Ritchie, Susan Sharbaugh, John Shook, John Wright and members of Boreal Partners in Flight for valuable information and conversation on Alaskan birds.

We are very grateful to David Sibley for his wonderful illustrations. Many thanks to Rick Ernst and Dave Porter for information on birding in Denali State Park and on the south side of the Alaska Range. Also, thanks to Fred Dean for his comments on changes along the Denali Park Road, Kenneth Kertell for text from the original *Bird-Finding Guide to Denali*, and Peter Dunne and Stan Senner for reviewing the manuscript.

Coordinator: Charlie Loeb
Designer: Carole Thickstun
Editor: Nora L. Deans

Library of Congress Control Number: 2001 134024

Published by the Alaska Natural History Association,
750 West Second Avenue Suite 100, Anchorage, Alaska 99501.
1-866-AKPARKS

NATURAL HISTORY ASSOCIATION

www.alaskanha.org

Printed in the United States.
ISBN 0-930931-38-6

TABLE OF CONTENTS

*Phylogenetic sequence and nomenclature follow the American
Ornithologists' Union Checklist of North American Birds, 7th ed.,
and supplements.*

 National Park and
Preserve is best known for its outstanding scenery and unparalleled
opportunities for seeing grizzlies, moose, caribou, sheep and wolves.
But the national park and its surrounding region offer so much more . . .
botanical treasures, geological wonders, anadromous and resident fishes,
swarming populations of invertebrates and birds from all over the world.

You can't help but notice the diversity of birds living within this magnificent scenery. Denali National Park encompasses nearly six million acres of a
subarctic ecosystem, of which about 17 percent is covered year-round with
ice and snow. The remaining acreage provides important breeding, migratory
stopover and wintering habitat for more than 165 species of birds. Some,
like boreal chickadees and common redpolls, live here throughout the cold,
dark, long winter. Well-adapted for surviving in freezing conditions, they are
joined in spring by migrants from around the world. By late May, Denali
species "rub shoulders" with northern wheatears from Africa, arctic terns
from Antarctic waters, and long-tailed jaegers from the Pacific Ocean.

While Alaska is home to many organisms, it is a common
misconception that it "teems with wildlife." The entrance to Denali National
Park sits at nearly 64° North latitude, and here you'll see fewer species of
birds than in more southerly habitats or in the rich coastal habitats of
southern and western Alaska. Denali birding rewards not by force of
numbers, but in the spare elegance of the far north and its denizens, held
within the supernal light. Here you'll encounter the drab shorebirds of
coastal passage in full breeding plumage. The long-tailed jaeger, glimpsed as
only a gray shadow on a California pelagic trip, catches your eye in Denali

hawking insects on the tundra or swiftly swooping to snatch a vole off the ground.

The ranges of many northern birds extend around the top of the world, especially those of the order *Charadriiformes*, which includes the plover family *(Charadriidae)*, the sandpiper and phalarope family *(Scolopacidae)*, and the gulls, terns and jaeger family *(Laridae)*. The farther north you go, of course, the shorter the circle you make around the globe. Not surprisingly, the northernmost breeders tend to be the most circumpolar; in fact, most breeding birds of the highest latitudes are found all over the Arctic. Cape Morris Jesup on Greenland is the northern extreme of land, and the extreme of avian breeding. The birds found there, like the arctic tern and the long-tailed jaeger, are inveterate world travelers that also breed in Denali.

Denali Birds

This book covers about 25 percent of the species that occur in Denali. These species are a cross-section of Denali's diverse avifauna. Some are species that draw birders to Alaska because of their rarity in North America. Others are residents included because their life histories teach us about physiological adaptations to life in the far north. We included long- and short-distance migratory birds because they illustrate the connection between Denali and the rest of the world. Collectively, these species exemplify the global avian community of Denali and emphasize the challenges facing all of Denali's birds.

The tremendous growth of human populations and the even greater growth in resource consumption destroy and alter habitats, food supplies and introduce deadly chemicals into our environment. Years ago, many people in North America heeded the words of Rachel Carson and took dramatic steps to eliminate some of the chemicals threatening bird populations. But today, the threat of a silent spring—a world devoid of the glorious songs of birds—is still escalating because of human environmental impacts that are spreading to remote places like Denali. By understanding the ecological threats facing Denali's birds, perhaps we can more clearly see our role in preserving global ecosystems for the birds, and for ourselves.

Birding in Denali

Many opportunities await birders in Denali. Most of Denali is only accessible by foot, but several roads offer access to a variety of habitats. The 90-mile (145-kilometer) Denali Park Road bisects taiga, tundra and alpine habitats through Denali National Park on the north side of the Alaska Range. The park road is primarily accessed by shuttle and tour buses, although you may drive a private vehicle to the Savage River at mile 14.8 or ride a bicycle any distance. There are several campgrounds along the park road and in local communities, and you can camp in the backcountry. The George Parks Highway (State Highway #3) provides access to good birding areas along the eastern boundary of the national park. Denali State Park is also a great place for birdwatching on the south side of the Alaska Range, and the Petersville Road near Trapper Creek provides access to many good birding areas. Readers will quickly become aware that we focus almost exclusively on birding during the breeding season. Birding in winter also has its rewards, especially in late March and April when the sun returns to this area. But be prepared for foul weather and short bird lists! No matter where you venture in Denali, you're sure to find plenty of places to watch, study and enjoy Denali's birds.

A Few Cautionary Remarks

While birding in Denali, you may encounter bears, wolves and moose. Caution prevails in such situations and we encourage you to consult the *Denali Alpenglow* or a National Park Service ranger or a tour or shuttle bus driver for recommended behavior around these animals.

We deliberately omitted traditional nest sites from this book. National Park Service guidelines request that you stay at least 300 feet (100 meters) away from the nests of raptors or ground-nesting birds. If your presence alters the behavior of the birds you're watching, leave the area quickly so that the birds may get back to their daily routines. Please do not enter nesting areas. By keeping nesting birds away from or off of their nests, you increase the chances of them abandoning their nesting effort.

During your stay in Denali, keep in mind the wise words of naturalist Terry McEneaney, *"anyone can watch birds, but the true birder has the ability and experience to observe birds without disrupting them."* Finally, please respect Denali and all its treasures so other visitors can continue to enjoy Denali as one of the greatest places on Earth.

COMMON LOON
Gavia immer

The common loon has one of nature's most haunting voices, which you can hear in Denali's Lake country where the loons raise their broods. Loons spend most of their lives on water, coming ashore only to breed. They build their nests from vegetation on shorelines or islands of lakes and ponds. Loons are well-equipped to catch many species of their main diet, fish, which groups them with other fish-eating birds known as *piscivores*. The loon's solid bones help it approximate specific water gravity, and by expelling air in its feathers and lungs, the loon sinks beneath the water's surface. These skilled divers can stay under water for nearly a minute and may reach depths of 240 feet (75 meters). Loons are some of the oldest living birds on Earth. Their fossils date back at least 65 million years.

MIGRATION: Common loons from Alaska usually winter from the Aleutian Islands south to Baja California. They also winter on larger inland lakes along the Pacific Coast of the United States. Their migration routes are not fully known, although most birds probably migrate close to the coasts.

CONSERVATION STATUS: Long regarded as barometers of environmental quality due to their position on the top of the aquatic food chain, common loons could soon be the new "canary in the coal mine" for aquatic environments. While human activity has reduced the abundance and breeding range of the common loon, new research suggests that environmental pollutants such as mercury could threaten the long-term viability of common loons in northern ecosystems. Loons face a full suite of other threats associated with human activities, including loss of shoreline habitat, disturbance caused by motorized boats (outboard motors are particularly bad for loons; jet-skis are even worse), lake acidification, injuries and mortality from fishing line and hooks, lead poisoning from ingesting lead sinkers, and environmental pollution on their coastal wintering grounds. Many conservation efforts are currently underway to maintain loon habitat and decrease threats to loons across North America.

DENALI HABITAT: Larger lakes; loons are therefore easier to see on the south side of the Alaska Range.

LOCATIONS: Wonder Lake in Denali National Park; Byers Lake, Lake Denali, Swan Lake, and other large lakes in and around Denali State Park.

Trumpeter Swan
Cygnus buccinator

Weighing in at 21 to 30 pounds (10 to 14 kilograms), trumpeter swans are the largest waterfowl in North America and the largest swan in the world. As you may have guessed, the trumpeter swan is named for its resonant, trumpet-like call. Although once fairly common throughout most of northern North America, market hunting and the millinery trade drastically reduced populations during the ninteenth century. By the late 1800s, the species appeared to be extinct. In 1932, a small non-migratory population of 69 individuals was discovered in the Greater Yellowstone Ecosystem. To protect this remnant, the U.S. Fish and Wildlife Service established Red Rock Lakes National Wildlife Refuge in Montana's Centennial Valley.

Trumpeter swans were first identified in Alaska in 1850, but it wasn't until 1954 that breeders were discovered in the state. In 1968, this species was removed from the Federal Endangered Species List, but it is still rare or endangered in some states. Today, as a result of an intensive international conservation effort, the once nearly extinct trumpeter swan population is increasing. Surveys conducted by the U.S. Fish and Wildlife Service since 1968 show a 535 percent increase in the number of trumpeter swans in North America. Surveys in 2000 found nearly 24,000 trumpeter swans in North America. Trumpeter swans breeding in Alaska belong to the Pacific

Coast population, which currently numbers about 17,500 birds (or about 75 percent of the world population). Surveys in Denali in August 2000 yielded 922 adults and 223 young.

MIGRATION: Trumpeter swans that breed in Alaska winter in southeast coastal Alaska and south to Washington. They begin arriving along the British Columbia coast about November 1, with peak numbers seen in January and early February. Spring migration for the Pacific Coast population starts in mid- to late February. By mid-March, most of these swans have left coastal areas, but they don't appear on the Alaska breeding grounds until mid- to late April. After the swans leave their wintering grounds, they cross the Coast Mountains of British Columbia and head north, stopping at large lakes in central British Columbia and southern Yukon along the way. Birders interested in seeing large congregations of swans in migration should visit Marsh Lake near Whitehorse, Yukon, in mid-April.

CONSERVATION: Overall, the outlook for trumpeter swans looks bright. However, the National Audubon's Society's WatchList rates them as a moderate priority, and there are still serious threats to these populations, most of all habitat loss. While the Pacific Coast population is currently increasing and expanding its range, human activities in productive lowland areas of Alaska and in its wintering areas are increasing. Swans are very sensitive to disturbance and may have an unsuccessful breeding season if high levels of human activity occur near their chosen nesting site.

DENALI HABITAT: Freshwater marshes, ponds, lakes and large, slow-flowing rivers.

LOCATIONS: Very common south of the Alaska Range and in the Minchumina Basin region of Denali National Park. Seen occasionally at Wonder Lake and on large shallow tundra ponds west of Eielson Visitor Center during spring and fall migration. Denali State Park at Byers Lake, Indian River area and sloughs of the Tokositna River. Otto Lake, and Stampede Road. South of Denali State Park at Swan Lake and other lakes.

TUNDRA SWAN
Cygnus columbianus

Once known as the whistling swan in North America, the adult tundra swan's voice is higher pitched and less resonant than that of the trumpeter swan. Over 75 percent of North America's tundra swans nest on the treeless arctic plains of northern and western Alaska. This swan is more common and widespread than the trumpeter swan in North America. Unlike the trumpeter, tundra swans never declined to the point of extinction, and increases in their populations allow for limited hunting by permit.

MIGRATION: Tundra swans migrate in family groups along traditional routes across North America. Young tundra swans must make many stops to rest and feed during the autumn migration, so suitable habitat along their route is important for their survival. Two separate wintering populations of tundra swans live in Alaska. Swans from western Alaska (south of Point Hope) usually winter on the Pacific coast while swans from northern Alaska (east of Point Hope) migrate across the North American continent to spend the winter on the Atlantic coast. The north side of the Alaska Range is a major flyway for migrating tundra swans from the Yukon-Kuskokwim river deltas.

Research studies by U.S. Geological Survey scientists indicate that tundra swans breeding on the Yukon-Kuskokwim Delta migrate inland along a trans-Rocky Mountain route from Alaska to Montana, Idaho, Utah and Nevada during fall and spring migration to and from their coastal wintering grounds in central California.

CONSERVATION: The loss of aquatic habitat along migratory routes and wintering areas has forced tundra and trumpeter swans to use farmlands more often during migration and over winter. This raises questions concerning the effect of agricultural chemicals on swan populations and the effect of swans on the farmland. Oil and gas drilling and related activities pose potential threats to arctic breeding habitats of tundra swans. Also, mortality from lead poisoning and both regulated and unregulated hunting pose concerns. Intensive international cooperation will be needed to protect and preserve tundra and trumpeter swans in the future.

DENALI HABITAT: Lakes, ponds, and slow-moving rivers.

LOCATIONS: Seen in the Denali area during spring and fall migration. No breeding occurs in this area.

HARLEQUIN DUCK
Histrionicus histrionicus

Harlequin ducks spend most of their lives at sea, coming inland to breed along swift, clear mountain streams. The envy of many whitewater enthusiasts, harlequins ride the rapids of torrent streams, effortlessly maneuvering through boulder fields and gushing water in search of prey. Harlequins pair up during the non-breeding season and usually arrive on their breeding grounds as mated pairs. These beautiful ducks are a welcome sight each spring. It is not uncommon to see several pairs near the Savage River bridge in early June. The colorful male spends very little time there, returning to sea as soon as the female begins incubation.

Harlequins that breed inland have split personalities when it comes to food. During the breeding season they feed extensively on bottom-dwelling invertebrates and when available, fish eggs. During the non-breeding season, harlequins eat intertidal invertebrates, such as snails, limpets, crabs, chitons and mussels, as well as herring spawn.

MIGRATION: The exact migration routes of harlequins from interior Alaska is not documented. Harlequins winter in the Aleutian Islands, Kodiak Archipelago, Prince William Sound, and along the Pacific Coast to northern California.

CONSERVATION: The life history characteristics of harlequin ducks make them vulnerable to environmental disturbance. They live long, mature late and produce few young. Harlequin ducks depend on oxygen-rich streams during the breeding season and productive nearshore coastal areas during the non-breeding season. Known threats to wintering areas include high vulnerability to oil pollution and habitat alteration. We should never forget the impact of the *Exxon Valdez* oil spill of 1989 on harlequin ducks and other wildlife in Prince William Sound. Scientists estimate that between 1,200 to 2,500 harlequin ducks died as a direct result of the spill. Scientists with the U.S. Geological Survey and Oregon State University examined the survival of harlequins in both oiled and un-oiled areas of Prince William Sound. Their studies indicate that harlequin ducks were exposed to residual *Exxon Valdez* oil as many as nine years after the spill, and that ducks overwintering in areas exposed to oil had lower survival rates than ducks living in oil-free areas. Because adult survival rate directly impacts population dynamics of harlequin ducks, we must have the foresight to protect these coastal regions from oil spills and other human-caused environmental disturbances.

DENALI HABITAT: Swift, productive, clear streams.

LOCATIONS: Lower Caribou Creek just south of the Savage River bridge on the Denali Park Road, Savage River, Igloo Creek, Stony Creek, Moose Creek, and Byers and Troublesome Creeks in Denali State Park.

LONG-TAILED DUCK
Clangula hyemalis

The exuberant yodels of the long-tailed duck (formerly oldsquaw) ringing out across its circumpolar breeding range to nearly 82° N are sure signs that summer is on the way. This handsome duck is one of the most common of the arctic ducks, but very little is known about their basic breeding biology. It is one of a suite of sea ducks that breeds in Denali. Long-tailed ducks sometimes build their nests near those of arctic terns, perhaps since arctic terns are very aggressive when predators approach and usually drive them away by dive-bombing and vocalizing. Long-tailed ducks are very efficient divers. Scientists have recorded them feeding at depths of up to 180 feet (55 meters), and found that they commonly feed at depths of 90 to 150 feet (27 to 45 meters). Like many sea ducks, males leave the breeding grounds soon after clutches are completed. "Flotillas" of males are commonly observed on rivers and along the coastline of Alaska in late June and July.

MIGRATION: Long-tailed ducks from Alaska spend much of their lives at sea, wintering in areas along the Pacific Coast, Bering Sea, Sea of Okhotsk and Sea of Japan.

CONSERVATION: The U.S. Fish and Wildlife Service reports a decline in populations of long-tailed ducks in the tundra habitat zones on the Yukon-Kuskokwim river deltas and on wintering areas at sea. The decline may be linked to lead poisoning on the breeding grounds, environmental contaminants (such as cadmium, selenium and hydrocarbons) in marine ecosystems, unsustainable harvests across their range in Russia, and changes in winter food abundance and availability due to oceanic warming. Long-tailed ducks are listed on the Audubon WatchList for Alaska because of their declining populations and threats to their staging and wintering grounds.

DENALI HABITAT: While spending most of their lives at sea, long-tailed ducks breed inland across coastal and interior Alaska around ponds and lakes and along river estuaries and lagoons.

LOCATIONS: Long-tailed ducks have become difficult to find in Denali. Tundra ponds along the Wonder Lake road remain the best locale. They are seen in migration at Byers Lake.

DAS 2000

BARROW'S GOLDENEYE
Bucephala islandica

Starting life by tumbling through the air as they leave the safety of their nest, Barrow's goldeneye chicks hit the water and are on their way. Both Barrow's and common goldeneyes have very stiff wings, creating a whistling sound as they fly overhead. No surprise that they've long been known to birders and waterfowl enthusiasts as "whistle wings."

Barrow's goldeneyes commonly nest in cavities, and more uncommonly under rocks and brush and along stream banks. In *Birds of Mt. McKinley*, Adolph Murie describes a female goldeneye that kept lighting on the stone pipe at the Igloo Creek cabin. Murie presumes that she was investigating the pipe as a potential nest site! These birds exhibit very strong nest site fidelity. Females often return to the same nest site year after year, especially after successfully raising a brood. In fact, female Barrow's goldeneyes will start prospecting for nest sites during the fall before they migrate. Female offspring will often return to areas very close to their natal areas to breed. Courtship and pair bonding is well underway in late winter, with multiple males displaying around individual females.

MIGRATION: Barrow's goldeneyes breed in widely separated areas in western and northwestern North America, Quebec, Labrador and Greenland. Birds winter along both coasts and also on inland lakes and rivers. In Alaska, Barrow's goldeneyes winter regularly in large numbers in Prince William Sound.

CONSERVATION: Barrow's goldeneyes regularly winter at sea and are thus susceptible to changes in food supplies caused by environmental and human-induced factors as well as environmental pollutants.

DENALI HABITAT: Lakes, ponds and oxbow sloughs in the Denali area.

LOCATIONS: Big Railroad Lake; Horseshoe Lake in Denali National Park; in small ponds in Denali State Park, including beaver ponds at the start of the Little Coal Creek Trail.

NORTHERN GOSHAWK
Accipiter gentilis

"A shadow cast in gray, with piercing red eyes that radiate malevolence . . . In the north, in winter, prey is scarce. Something that moves lives. Something that lives may escape, but not from a goshawk." Pete Dunne so aptly describes the largest of North America's three accipiters. Goshawks are extremely aggressive hunters; they often chase prey in an "all-out aerial sprint," as Dunne would say, and will crash through thick brush in pursuit of their prey on foot. Goshawks breeding at high latitudes are opportunistic hunters and have broad diets, consisting mainly of medium-sized mammals and medium to large birds. Their catch depends on the season and the vulnerability and abundance of prey.

MIGRATION: In most years, Northern goshawks are one of the few raptors that may overwinter in the Denali area. They are particularly common in years when showshoe hare populations are high. Most reside throughout their breeding range, but a small portion of the population, usually juveniles, regularly winters away. However, in years of prey scarcity, even the adults move south in an "invasion." For instance, at Kluane in the Yukon Territory, goshawks are year-round residents when snowshoe hares are abundant, but they leave the area when hares decline. This is probably true in Denali and other northern breeding areas as well. Little is known about the winter ecology of this species in North America.

CONSERVATION: Current management concerns over northern goshawks in North America are similar to those raised by the northern spotted owl (*Strix occidentalis caurina*) a decade ago. The northern goshawk is listed as a "watch" species by the U.S. Fish and Wildlife Service. Due to the protected status of goshawks and the increasing concern about their population status, researchers are studying habitat characteristics and the impact of land management activities. Recent evidence suggests that populations of goshawks are declining, particularly in the western United States, and habitat alteration by timber harvesting is one of the most significant factors. Sensitive to habitat change, these predators are considered "management indicator" species in many national forests. Estimates of population size are difficult because extensive nest searches are needed over very large, remote areas, and these wary birds do not nest close together.

SPECIAL CAUTION: During the breeding season, goshawks are very aggressive and have little tolerance for intruders near the nest. Unwary birdwatchers are greeted with low, swift, dive-bombs and blood-curdling alarm calls. As some park visitors can testify, getting too close to a nest may result in wounds from a powerful blow to the head.

DENALI HABITAT: Northern goshawks are associated with forests and woodlands throughout their range.

LOCATIONS: Park headquarters, Teklanika Forest, and other mixed-forested areas. Visitors in Denali are most likely to see goshawks flying or soaring over forested areas.

GOLDEN EAGLE
Aquila chrysaetos

Soaring silently along hillsides or high above the tundra, or perched on the skyline of the Alaska Range foothills, the golden eagle is well known to all below it. Lambs of Dall's sheep scurry back to their mothers, and arctic ground squirrels high-tail it back to their burrows in the shadow of the golden eagle. These large birds frequent the skies of Denali from late February to early October. If prey is sufficient, some may overwinter. Early in spring, the skies fill with wildly undulating, acrobatic eagles marking their territorial boundaries. As eagles patrol their territories, they are often mobbed by gyrfalcons, merlins, magpies and even smaller birds. While this harrassment doesn't seem to provoke the eagles, smaller mobbers could easily become a mid-day snack for the eagle. Later in the spring, nonbreeding adult and subadult eagles, or "floaters," pass through the area, often pursued by territorial eagles.

Building their nests on cliffs and rock outcrops in Denali, eagles lay eggs in early to mid-April, when temperatures rarely climb above freezing. The eggs hatch 45 days later. By late July and early August, recently fledged eaglets join the sky patrol as they gain flying experience and hone their hunting skills. The remains of almost every terrestrial vertebrate, with the exception of moose and grizzly, have been found in golden eagle nests in Denali. Their mainstay here is snowshoe hare, ptarmigan, arctic ground squirrel and hoary marmot. Like many northern predators, the reproductive cycles of Denali's golden eagles are tied to the snowshoe hare cycle. Denali's eagles know few predators other than humans and other eagles. However, grizzlies have successfully raided golden eagle nests.

MIGRATION: Most golden eagles from Denali are migratory. They depart Denali in late September, flying southeast through Alaska and southern Yukon and continuing southward through British Columbia, Alberta and Saskatchewan. Juveniles reach their wintering areas in early to late November. Many of Denali's golden eagles overwinter along the Front Range of the Rocky Mountains, northern Great Plains and northern Mexico. Autumn and spring migration routes are similar, but adults depart their wintering areas and return to Alaska much earlier than subadults or juveniles.

CONSERVATION: Many northern breeding areas are relatively unaltered and protected. Wintering populations, however, encounter illegal shooting, poisoning, electrocution, disturbance and decreasing prey populations resulting from habitat alteration.

SPECIAL CAUTION: Golden eagles are particularly sensitive to human disturbance in the breeding season. Visitors are cautioned to stay away from nests.

DENALI HABITAT: Mountainous and open habitat. As Pete Dunne says, "golden eagles prefer terrain at odds with the horizon."

LOCATIONS: Northeastern portion of Denali contains a dense breeding population. Sightings are common in mountainous regions. Also seen in Denali State Park on Curry and Kesugi Ridges and in the Peters Hills.

MERLIN
Falco columbarius

A fierce, small falcon, the merlin breeds in the boreal forest of North America. Found in good numbers in Denali, some of the most intensive research on merlins in northern latitudes has been conducted here. Like other falcons, merlins don't build their own nests. They find nests originally built by black-billed magpies or nest on the ground in shrubby areas. Nest sites are usually found near riparian zones. Males often perch on neighboring trees or shrubs as they guard their nests from other birds or mammals. You may also spot them dashing along the treeline in search of prey. In Denali, merlins often hunt in alpine areas, traveling many miles away from their nesting areas. Exceptionally fast and agile, merlins out-maneuver most of their aerial prey, snapping up passerines, dragonflies and other insects in the blink of an eye.

MIGRATION: Merlins are complete migrants in interior Alaska and winter from southern California to northern South America. Breeders return to Denali in mid- to late April to set up territories.

CONSERVATION: Environmental contaminants, including DDE, a residue of DDT, have been found in merlin eggs in Denali. This pesticide causes reproductive dysfunctions, such as thin eggshells. Although most merlins in Denali are not affected by pesticide contamination and are reproducing well, some individuals may still be impacted.

SPECIAL CAUTION: Merlins vigorously defend their territories and will dive repeatedly at threatening mammals and birds. You should remain at least 300 feet (100 meters) away from occupied nests to avoid disturbing nesting birds. You should NEVER approach a ground nest, as you may lead predators, like red foxes, to these vulnerable nest sites.

DENALI HABITAT: Nests in a variety of habitats from spruce forests to open shrubby tundra. Hunts mainly over open habitats, including alpine areas.

LOCATIONS: Merlins are observed frequently along the Denali Park Road, especially near the Savage and Sanctuary River Campgrounds and in Igloo Forest. They are infrequently seen in the Veteran's Memorial and Byers Lake area of Denali State Park and the Susitna River area around Trapper Creek. Keep a keen ear out for the merlin's high pitched "ki-ki-kee" calls, as these birds are sometimes easier to find by sound rather than by sight.

GYRFALCON AND GOLDEN EAGLE

GYRFALCON
Falco rusticolus

Elusive, powerful and well-adapted for life in the Arctic, gyrfalcons are the largest falcon in the world. However, we understand little about the ecology of this species because they live in remote and rugged areas. From late February through early October, gyrfalcons share the Denali skies with a large breeding population of golden eagles. If you're patient and lucky, you might be rewarded with a front-row seat for an aerial dog-fight between these two large raptors.

Gyrfalcons are true arctic falcons; they breed throughout the north latitudes and only leave as adults if food is scarce. Extremely powerful fliers, they'll chase down ptarmigan and other prey. As they hunt, you can almost hear them calling out "resistance is futile." During the breeding season, gyrfalcons prey heavily on arctic ground squirrels, ptarmigan and an occasional snowshoe hare. In winter, they rely heavily on ptarmigan.

Gyrfalcons often use nests originally built by golden eagles or ravens. Falcons lay their eggs in late March, when daily temperatures rarely rise above freezing. The nestlings fledge by mid- to late July. Like golden eagles and ravens, incubating gyrfalcons must endure late winter and early spring snowstorms.

MIGRATION: Gyrfalcons are one of the few raptors that regularly overwinter in Denali. Adults are more likely to overwinter than juveniles, and depend heavily on ptarmigan for survival during the winter. We know little about their non-breeding season movements in Alaska. Limited research suggests that juveniles leave their natal areas in mid- to late September and often move long distances in search of prey.

CONSERVATION: Northern breeding areas are relatively unaltered, but increased hunting pressures on ptarmigan may locally influence gyrfalcon populations. There are concerns for gyrfalcons that overwinter in Russia due to trapping pressures, habitat alteration and environmental contaminants.

SPECIAL CAUTION: Gyrfalcons are particularly sensitive to human disturbance in the breeding season. Visitors are cautioned to stay away from occupied nests.

DENALI HABITAT: Mountainous and remote areas.

LOCATIONS: Denali hosts a large breeding population and sightings are common in mountainous regions along the Park Road corridor, especially near Polychrome, Stony Hill and Thorofare Ridge. You are most likely to see gyrfalcons flying overhead or perched on rock outcrops.

PTARMIGAN
(*Lagopus* spp.)

You can see all three species of North American ptarmigan species in Denali . . . if you work hard enough. In summer, these species are layered like a cake according to habitat, size and abundance. The smallest and least abundant white-tailed ptarmigan (*Lagopus leucurus*) prefer steep slopes and ridges above the brushline. The larger and more abundant rock ptarmigan (*L. mutus*) occupy moderately sloping ground just above timberline. The largest and most abundant willow ptarmigan (*L. lagopus*) live below timberline.

Of the three, willow ptarmigan are the easiest to see in Denali. Territorial males perch atop willows and smaller spruce trees in spring, their cackling calls bursting across the landscape. Later in summer, wary parents herd large broods along the Denali Park Road. Observing rock ptarmigan takes a bit more work, but a day trip to the Cathedral or Igloo Mountain area may result in discovery of "rockers." White-tailed ptarmigan generate the most sweat, as birders need to hike above 3,500 feet (1,000 meters) to see them.

In winter, snow depth and availability of food dictates the distribution of all three species. Mixed flocks are not uncommon in winter, when you might also see goshawks and gyrfalcons chasing flocks of ptarmigan.

MIGRATION: All three species are resident. Local movements occur in winter as flocks seek out food and shelter.

CONSERVATION: Similar to snowshoe hare, ptarmigan populations are famous for great variation in abundance. Populations vary between super-abundant to nearly absent in just a few years. Local populations are assumed healthy and self-sustaining. However, we don't know how persistent organic pollutants affect ptarmigan populations in Alaska.

DENALI HABITAT: As described above.

LOCATIONS: Varies seasonally. In summer, willow ptarmigan are commonly seen at lower elevations along the Denali Park Road. Rock ptarmigan are commonly found at elevations greater than 3,000 feet (915 meters) on Cathedral Mountain, Primrose Ridge and in the Kantishna Hills. White-tailed ptarmigan are found at higher elevations and near permanent snowfields, such as the ridges separating the Toklat and Stony Creek drainages. In winter, mixed flocks are seen at lower elevations.

SANDHILL CRANE
Grus canadensis

As the snowline and temperatures drop, and the tundra turns crimson and gold, large flocks of sandhill cranes whirl overhead on their way south. Through mid-September, listen for the loud, resonating "garroo-garroo-garroo" of adults and the higher-pitched, whistle-like calls of juveniles. A loose fusion of several flocks may number up to hundreds of individuals and thousands may pass through Denali in a single day. Flying in V-formation, large flocks unchain as individual cranes spiral upwards on thermals and air currents, often gaining thousands of feet of altitude before continuing on their southward movements. Many of these cranes originate in the Kuskokwim and Yukon river country and others may be from as far away as eastern Russia.

MIGRATION: The lesser sandhill cranes we see on the north side of the Alaska Range form the mid-continent population. These cranes winter in Texas, the southwestern United States and Mexico and use the Platte River in Nebraska during migration. Cranes breeding on the south side of the Alaska Range in the Susitna River drainage probably belong to the Pacific Flyway population and generally winter in the Central Valley of California.

CONSERVATION: Cranes concentrate at migratory staging areas and on the wintering grounds and are particularly vulnerable to loss of habitat along migration routes and on wintering areas. Habitat conservation in specific areas, such as the central Platte River Valley in Nebraska, is essential for the long-term viability of sandhill crane populations from Alaska.

DENALI HABITAT: Open marshy tundra and wetlands.

LOCATIONS: Breeding pairs are difficult to observe in Denali. In spring, large flocks pass just north of Healy and some congregate on farm fields in the Trapper Creek area. In fall, large flocks pass over Wonder Lake, Stampede Road, the eastern Kantishna Hills and eastward along Denali's northern boundary. Flocks of cranes passing in front of snow-covered peaks of the Alaska Range is truly a memorable Denail experience.

American Golden-Plover
Pluvialis dominica

Exquisite plumage, evocative voice and globe-spanning reach make this species unsurpassed in sheer attractiveness. A wide range of invertebrates forms the bulk of the diet in the park, but crowberries and blueberries are important in the spring and fall. Until 1993, the American golden-plover was conspecific with the Pacific golden-plover (*Pluvialis fulva*), which nests in western and southwestern Alaska; consequently, we know less than we might about the behavior and distribution of either form. Early observers, including Adolph Murie, identified local birds as *Oulva*; however, no good record for this species exists in Denali. The closest known breeding populations of Pacific golden-plovers are on the Seward Peninsula and northwest of Lake Iliamna. Birders are urged to study golden-plovers in Alaska carefully.

MIGRATION: Of all the shorebirds, the American and Pacific golden-plovers perhaps best embody the term "wind birds" coined by author Peter Matthiessen. Migratory journeys of arctic nesting American golden-plovers are some of the longest of any of Earth's creatures. They often migrate more than 18,750 miles (30,000 kilometers) per year. While they are fast fliers, their journeys span immense distances and take many weeks to complete. They leave Alaska and head east across Canada to stage in northeastern Canada and the U.S. From there, a direct flight over the Atlantic Ocean to northeastern South America is the most common flight path. Most American golden-plovers winter in the pampas of Argentina and Uruguay. In spring, migrants head back to Alaska more directly by traveling along the Andes northward across Central America and the Great Plains and north to Alaska.

CONSERVATION: Like the Eskimo curlew and other shorebirds, the American golden-plover was heavily hunted for the marketplace in the nineteenth and early twentieth centuries. Once this pressure was lifted, the population rebounded somewhat, although loss of winter habitat likely prohibits a return to former abundance. Breeding habitat is still essentially undeveloped in the north, but winter grounds and migration stopovers are more vulnerable.

DENALI HABITAT: Dry to moist tundra of gently sloping uplands or flats, often rocky or hummocky.

LOCATIONS: Upper Primrose Ridge, upper Highway Pass, Little Stony flats, river benches of Toklat and Plains of Murie; Curry and Kesugi Ridges in Denali State Park; Peters Hills.

DAS 2000

WANDERING TATTLER
Heteroscelus incanus

Wandering tattlers are one of the species birders most often seek at Denali. The gray plumage of tattlers blends in well with their surroundings, but persistent birders are likely to find these beautiful shorebirds foraging along the edges of clear, gravelly mountain streams. Like several other "high-profile" species, little is known about the ecology of wandering tattlers in Alaska, and there are very few published studies on this species in North America.

Arriving in Denali in late May, tattlers set up nesting areas on gravel bars and stream sides in subalpine and alpine areas. Olaus and Adolph Murie made the first scientific observation of a wandering tattler nest on a gravel bar along the Savage River on July 1, 1923.

MIGRATION: By mid-August, Denali's tattlers are on their way back to their wintering grounds. Many tattlers winter along the Pacific Coast from southern California to Mexico, but others are trans-oceanic migrants wintering in the South Pacific on the Hawaiian and Philippine islands and in Australia.

CONSERVATION: The Alaska Shorebird Working Group considers the wandering tattler a shorebird of high conservation concern in interior Alaska because of the importance of Alaska to their populations. The wandering tattler is probably one of the least populous shorebird species in North America, and Alaska is the principal breeding area for the species. In winter, tattlers are found on gravel tidal flats and rocky shores. These areas are vulnerable to oil pollution and human encroachment.

DENALI HABITAT: Riverine alluvia and gravel shorelines.

LOCATIONS: Savage River upstream from the Denali Park Road bridge; Igloo Creek and its tributaries, particularly Tattler Creek; Stony and Little Stony Creeks.

WHIMBREL
Numenius phaeopus

Large and vocal whimbrels are most often seen and heard in Denali in early to mid-May when they return to their breeding grounds. Whimbrels are the widest ranging of the curlew genus. Whimbrels may have been more common in Denali in the early twentieth century when scientists Joseph Dixon and Adolph Murie found this species nesting in open tundra areas along the Denali Park Road. Dixon and Murie found whimbrels nesting close by long-tailed jaegers in Denali and speculated that both species benefited from each other's nest vigilance. Whimbrels keep close watch on their nests and are very vocal when intruders are near. Jaegers are territorial and drive intruders from their nesting areas.

More recent observations along the park road by long-term park observers suggest that whimbrels have declined in this area. We don't know exactly why, but suspect changes in vegetation, the drainage regime along the park road, increases in road traffic and increases in human activities.

MIGRATION: Whimbrels nest in two widely separated areas in North America—in Alaska and the Yukon, and west and south of Hudson Bay. Biologists suggest that these populations fly down the west and east coasts, respectively, and winter from Vancouver Island and South Carolina to Tierra del Fuego. Some birds may make long trans-oceanic flights; birds that stage in western Alaska are believed to migrate offshore to British Columbia.

CONSERVATION: Whimbrels were less hard-hit than some other shorebirds by the market hunting of the 1800s, thanks to their habitual wariness and their habit of forming smaller flocks during migration. Populations of whimbrels increased after the signing of the Convention for the Protection of Migratory Birds with Canada in 1916, but probably never reached former abundance. Destruction and degradation of this species' coastal habitat in winter is the greatest concern. Whimbrels are sensitive to disturbance at their nests and may abandon a nest after a single human visit. The Western Hemisphere Shorebird Reserve Network and the U.S. Shorebird Conservation Plan are attempting to recognize and protect the staging and wintering grounds of this species and other shorebirds.

DENALI HABITAT: Moist, tussocky tundra.

LOCATIONS: Primrose Ridge and tundra ponds west of Eielson Visitor Center in Denali National Park; Stampede Road; Curry and Kesugi Ridges above timberline in Denali State Park, including "Whimbrel Hill" overlooking Byers Lake; Peters Hills.

SURFBIRD
Aphriza virgata

One might wonder what a "surfbird" is doing in Denali. Like many other species, surfbirds spend a small portion of the year in Denali where they come to breed. They spend the remainder of their lives in coastal areas along rocky Pacific shorelines among the surf . . . hence their name. In Denali, these small, short-legged, rather stout birds share the alpine environment with northern wheatears, rock ptarmigan, long-tailed jaegers, horned larks and Dall sheep. Birders will delight in watching these beautiful, montane-breeding shorebirds scurrying across the tundra in search of insects.

George Wright made the first scientific observation of a surfbird nest on May 28, 1926. Wright and Joseph Dixon were making a biological reconnaissance of the fledgling Mt. McKinley National Park, when Wright made this famous discovery about 1,000 feet (300 meters) above timberline on a south-facing rocky ridge. Four years later, Wright became the first chief of the wildlife division of the National Park Service. Spurred on by his love of wild areas, Wright recognized early in the twentieth century that even large national parks were not biological islands isolated from the rest of the world. It seems only fitting that he would share in the discovery of a nest of a species that connects Denali to other parts of the world.

MIGRATION: Surfbirds leave Denali by late July on their way to their coastal wintering areas. The migratory routes and exact wintering areas of surfbirds from Denali are not known. In spring, surfbirds may stage in Prince William Sound.

CONSERVATION: Surfbirds connect Denali to coastal regions from Kodiak Island, Alaska, to the Strait of Magellan, Chile. The surfbird is listed on the National Audubon WatchList as a species of moderate conservation priority and by the Alaska Shorebird Conservation Plan as a species of high conservation priority. Threats include vulnerability of wintering and migratory stop-over habitat due to oil pollution, vulnerability to population declines due to small size of the population, and human encroachment along coastal wintering areas. According to Stan Senner, executive director of the Alaska State Office of the National Audubon Society, "Every aspect of surfbird biology and ecology needs further research. Only a handful of studies have focused on this species, and its basic breeding biology and behavior are among the most poorly known of any North American breeding shorebird."

DENALI HABITAT: Open alpine areas.

LOCATIONS: Primrose Ridge, Sable Pass, Stony Dome, Thorofare Ridge, upper Glacier Creek, Mount Galen, Kantishna Hills, Peters Hill.

COMMON SNIPE
Gallinago gallinago

The common snipe's "winnowing" is one of the most pervasive sounds heard at lower elevations in Denali from May to July. The winnowing comes from air flowing over stiff, outer tail feathers as the bird loses elevation in flight. It's the snipe's territorial advertisement on the breeding grounds. When you hear this winnowing, look up and you might spot one of these fat little birds flying erratically overhead.

Snipe are nearly impossible to see on the ground. They are relatively small and their cryptic plumage blends into the tundra. As you stroll through the tundra alert for bears, snipe will occasionally flush at your feet, exploding out of the vegetation and leaving you behind with your loudly thumping heart.

MIGRATION: The exact migration routes and wintering areas of snipe from Denali are not known. They probably winter from southern coastal Alaska, throughout North America and south through the Caribbean, Central America and northern South America.

CONSERVATION: Populations of this species appear stable. Known threats to snipe include the draining of wetlands on their wintering grounds.

DENALI HABITAT: Lowlands, including bogs and wet sedge tundra, where they probe peat-like soils in search of crane fly larvae and other invertebrate prey.

LOCATIONS: Tundra ponds, particularly along the Denali Park Road west of Eielson Visitor Center and in the fall in the Trapper Creek area.

RED-NECKED PHALAROPE
Phalaropus lobatus

Phalaropes have, as author Peter Matthiessen wrote, "carried their exchange of roles as far as their anatomy will permit." The larger, brighter females initiate courtship and have testosterone levels equal to males. One might accuse them of doing little but laying eggs, upon which they do not lower themselves to brood.

Phalaropes are the only regularly swimming shorebirds, and they spend most of their winter at sea. In summer, they are delightful to watch on the smaller ponds in Denail as they spin in tight circles creating vortex es that draw up insect larvae and crustaceans from the bottom of the pond. As prey rises to the top of the vortex, phalaropes are quick to grab and swallow their prey. These colorful, little birds often share their aquatic habitat with other species in Denali and a visit to one of the smaller ponds dotting the Denali landscape can yield great opportunities for studying foraging strategies. Arctic terns hover over and plunge into the pond in search of small fish, phalaropes spin madly around the shallower edges of the pond drawing up prey, and neighboring moose snorkel their way through the pond in search of aquatic vegetation.

MIGRATION: Red-necked phalaropes breed throughout the Arctic and winter at sea, mostly in the Southern Hemisphere. Nearctic birds are thought to spend the austral summer either in the Humboldt Current off South America, or, according to some authorities, off the East Indies.

CONSERVATION: Because phalaropes spend much of their lives at sea, they are susceptible to environmental contamination and changes in ocean conditions.

DENALI HABITAT: Freshwater ponds and margins of these ponds.

LOCATIONS: During spring migration and occasionally in mid-summer, phalaropes may be seen in ponds at the east end of the Park, or between Eielson Visitor Center and Wonder Lake.

LONG-TAILED JAEGER
Stercorarius longicaudus

Gracing the summer skies over Denali, long-tailed jaegers delight us with their aerial agility and beauty. Long-tailed jaegers are the smallest, most abundant and most northern of the jaegers in North America. While they are less powerful than other jaegers, they are very efficient predators of arthropods and smaller prey, including mice, voles, lemmings, and shrews. These small mammals comprise a large percentage of the summer diet of jaegers and influence jaeger reproductive success. More mice, voles, shrews and lemmings usually results in more jaeger fledglings. In years when these mammal populations are low, many jaegers will not breed at all. Instead, they'll make a living by eating arthropods, berries, fledgling songbirds, scavenging road-kill ground squirrels or stealing prey from other birds.

Unlike most bird species, female jaegers are larger than males. According to Klaus Olsen and Hans Larsson, who wrote a guide to the skuas and jaegers of the world, the reasons for this reversed sexual size dimorphism probably relate to their breeding strategy. The smaller, lighter males are better suited to hunting and the larger, heavier females are better suited for defending their nest and young. This seems to be an efficient adaptation, as long-tailed jaegers build their nest on the ground and must protect their eggs and young from a suite of predators, including red fox, wolverine and raptors.

MIGRATION: Long-tailed jaegers spend most of their lives at sea in the southern temperate oceans. Many are observed off southeast South America and off southwest Africa, but fewer in the southern Pacific Ocean. Watching long-tailed jaegers catch flying fishes is truly the sight of a lifetime!

CONSERVATION: Most long-tailed jaegers breed in remote areas. However, since jaegers feed high on the food chain and spend nearly 75 percent of their lives at sea, they are susceptible to long-lasting environmental contaminants, including DDT and its metabolites DDD and DDE and the industrial compound PCBs.

DENALI HABITAT: Dry or marshy tundra.

LOCATIONS: Upper Primrose Ridge; Sable Pass; Highway Pass to Eielson Visitor Center; Kesugi Ridge, Peters Hills.

ARCTIC TERN
Sterna paradisaea

Perhaps the most famous of all migrants, the quarter-pound arctic tern ranges from the extreme Arctic to the edge of the Antarctic pack ice, some making a round trip of over 25,000 miles (40,000 kilometers) each year. Of all animals, it probably enjoys the highest percentage of daylight in its life. They also live long; the oldest recorded arctic tern banded in North America lived for 34 years.

As agile and graceful as jaegers, these small terns are often seen in Denali as they hover seemingy effortlessly over ponds. With a quick motion, they pull in their wings, dive into the water, then fly off with prey in their bills. The tern's circumpolar breeding range dips to Washington state, where the first colony in the contiguous United States was discovered, and to Massachusetts.

MIGRATION: Terns migrate offshore over the Atlantic and Pacific Oceans. Large congregations winter around the pack-ice south of the Indian Ocean, although the birds disperse widely over the south seas, some flying east and circumnavigating the Antarctic. First-year birds do not make the trip back north to the Arctic; instead they spend the northern summer off the coast of Peru and Chile.

CONSERVATION: Globally, most breeding populations and breeding sites of arctic terns are not at risk. However, changes in ocean temperature and resulting changes in fisheries resources (small fishes and shrimp) may influence abundance and distribution of arctic terns over the next century. Because arctic terns spend so much of their lives at sea, oil spills and environmental contaminants are a cause for concern.

DENALI HABITAT: Breeds on the edges of lakes and ponds in Denali.

LOCATIONS: Wonder Lake; tundra ponds west of Eielson Visitor Center and near Wonder Lake, Byers Lakes, and lakes and ponds along Petersville Road, Chulitna and Susitna Rivers.

NORTHERN HAWK OWL
Surnia ulula

The probability of seeing one of these inquisitive owls in Denali often depends on being in the right place at the right time. The distribution and abundance of this species is somewhat unpredictable, but is probably most influenced by food supply. And like many species, hawk owls tend to move far and wide in search of food. While some areas almost always harbor an owl or two, hawk owls are difficult to find even in these areas when prey is scarce. It is often easier to find hawk owls in late winter and early spring in interior Alaska, as they move around in search of food, nest sites and mates. When present, owls can often be found by listening for their vocalizations or for the alarm calls of mobbing song birds.

Despite their popularity with birders, hawk owls are one of the least studied birds in North America. This is probably due to their very low densities and remoteness of their breeding areas. In the Old World, where hawk owls have been well studied, their abundance is tightly linked to the three- to four-year population cycles of voles. In the New World, where only a handful of studies exist, their abundance may be more influenced by the 8- to 11-year population cycle of snowshoe hares. While mice and voles may be the most commonly caught prey, hares may be brought to nests more often. Hares may be an even more important food source for hawk owls during winter.

MIGRATION: Northern hawk owls are nomadic; their movements probably correspond to regional food availability and climatic conditions. Irruptions of hawk owls into temperate latitudes are well known, but there are few quantitative studies on hawk owl movements. A female hawk owl banded near Edmonton, Alberta was recently found dead near Dillingham, Alaska, suggesting that these owls may move great distances.

CONSERVATION: The population dynamics and winter ecology of northern hawk owls are virtually unknown in North America. More than 50 percent of the northern hawk owl's North American breeding range occurs in noncommercial boreal forests. This owl only nests in cavities and hollow tops of trees. Forestry practices may reduce nest-site and hunting-perch availability, but may increase the abundance of small mammals. During the last century, northern hawk owl populations appeared secure in North America.

SPECIAL CAUTION: Northern hawk owls are exceptionally tolerant of humans. Because this species is highly sought after in Denali and birders may make repeated trips to a nesting area, the National Park Service requires that birders remain at least 300 feet (100 meters) away from nest sites during the nesting season to avoid disturbing these owls.

DENALI HABITAT: Isolated spruce stands, forest edges, and open canopy forests.

LOCATIONS: Forest edges along the Denali Park Road between Park Headquarters and the Teklanika River, and in the Kantishna area. South of Denali State Park in forests around Lake Denali and along Petersville Road and the Parks Highway. Most often seen perched near or on the top of trees and snags along a forest edge.

BOREAL OWL
Aegolius funereus

The characteristic soft song of interior Alaska's smallest owl is a true sign that spring is on its way. Heard more often than seen, you'll want to keep a keen ear for these calls in late March through early May when male owls are singing in hopes of finding a mate.

Boreal owls (Tengmalm's owl in the Old World) occupy boreal and subalpine forests across the world. They are obligate cavity nesters and often use cavities made by woodpeckers for nesting. Boreal owls prey mainly on small mammals, including voles and mice, but also prey on birds, insects and larger mammals, such as flying squirrels and young snowshoe hares. This species shows the most extreme reverse sexual size dimorphism of any North American owl—females are much larger than males.

MIGRATION: Boreal owls are nomadic throughout their range. They are generally year-round residents, but may disperse in years when food resources are scarce.

CONSERVATION: It is difficult to assess the conservation status of boreal owls because information about their basic life history is sparse. Reliable indications of long-term trends are unavailable because it is difficult to survey or census boreal owls. Concerns exist for populations of boreal owls in some areas, especially isolated montane populations south of the continuous boreal forest. Loss of natural breeding cavities or prey abundance may reduce breeding populations.

SPECIAL CAUTION: Boreal owls may nest in campgrounds and other developed areas in Denali. You should remain at least 300 feet (100 meters) from occupied nests to avoid disturbing nesting birds.

DENALI HABITAT: Boreal forest with black and white spruce, aspen, poplar and birch.

LOCATIONS: Forested areas near Park Headquarters, Savage River Campground, Igloo Forest and Toklat Ranger Cabin.

DAS 2000

THREE-TOED WOODPECKER
Picoides tridactylus

Of the five species of woodpeckers that are found in Denali, the three-toed woodpecker is often quiet, inconspicuous, and difficult to find. Its presence is often best revealed by a rapid and loud drumming as the bird hammers into trees in search of prey. This hardy woodpecker forages on insects in the bark of freshly killed trees and plays an important role in the control of a variety of forest insects, including bark beetles. Its range coincides with the distribution of spruce and other conifers throughout boreal forests and at high elevations in Eurasia and North America.

MIGRATION: The three-toed woodpecker is a year-round resident. Individuals will travel long distances to areas of insect infestations, such as burned or windfall areas in search of food.

CONSERVATION: The basic ecological requirements and population biology of this species are unknown. Its habitat is probably at risk in the western United States and Canada due to timber harvesting, salvage logging, firewood cutting, habitat fragmentation and suppression of wildfires. Periodic fires are probably important to this species—population densities increase during the first three years after a fire.

DENALI HABITAT: Mature boreal forests.

LOCATIONS: Mature forests along local roads in both Denali National Park and Denali State Parks.

OLIVE-SIDED FLYCATCHER
Contopus cooperi

Surprisingly little is known about the basic breeding biology of this easy to identify flycatcher. Best known for its "quick-three-beers" call, olive-sided flycatchers are heard throughout spruce forests at lower elevations in Denali. They habitually perch on the top of trees, particularly trees with dead tops, from which they launch to pursue prey, including wasps, yellow jackets and dragonflies. The birds return to their perches, prey in tow, where they kill their quarry by repeatedly striking it against the dead branches. Olive-sided flycatchers are very aggressive toward all intruders in their nesting areas and protect their nests vehemently against gray jays, red squirrels and other predators.

MIGRATION: Male olive-sided flycatchers arrive in interior Alaska in mid- to late May, with females arriving one to two weeks later. They depart interior Alaska mid- to late August and winter primarily from Central America to central South America.

CONSERVATION: Results from Breeding Bird Surveys indicate that this species has declined over much of North America. As a result, Boreal Partners in Flight lists olive-sided flycatchers as a species of concern. Impacts on the breeding grounds are not well-documented, but wintering habitat in South America has been heavily impacted by forestry.

DENALI HABITAT: Black spruce muskeg, dwarf coniferous forest, usually with a few larger trees in the area.

LOCATIONS: Park Headquarters area; Savage River; Triple Lakes; Wonder Lake and Kantishna area.

ALDER FLYCATCHER
Empidonax alnorum

The appreciation of *Empidonax* flycatchers may be an acquired taste, but once learned, it becomes powerfully addictive. Impossible to identify solely by sight in the field and in the hand, only the voice of the alder flycatcher is a sure-fire field mark. Their rapid, raspy songs (fee-bee-o) are innate and there are no confusing local dialects. Fortunately, the Hammond's flycatcher (*Empidonax hammondii*) can be identified by sight and the look-alike willow flycatcher (*E. trailii*) does not occur in Alaska. In spring, Hammond's flycathers arrive in Denail weeks earlier than alder flycatchers.

Through a long-term banding project at Creamer's Field in Fairbanks, Alaska, the Alaska Bird Observatory has uncovered some amazing facts about these insectivores. Alder flycatchers only spend about 48 days a year in Alaska, far less than other breeding birds in interior Alaska. They arrive just after the last freezing temperatures in spring, breed, raise young, and leave just before the first freezing temperatures in late summer. Unlike many long-distance migrants, alder flycatchers arrive and depart with little fat reserves and they do not molt on the breeding grounds. These data highlight the importance of local research on these long-distance migrants.

MIGRATION: Alder flycatchers spend most of their lives on their wintering grounds in northern South America.

CONSERVATION: There are no data available to determine the population status or conservation issues related to this species.

DENALI HABITAT: Thickets of alder, willow and other shrubs.

LOCATIONS: Alder flycatchers abound along the Petersville Road. Also look and listen for them at Wonder Lake and along the George Parks Highway between Trapper Creek and Denali State Park.

NORTHERN SHRIKE
Lanius excubitor

The northern shrike, the most widely distributed of all shrikes, breeds throughout the Arctic. In North America, the northern shrike breeds from western Alaska to Labrador. In Latin, *Lanius* means "butcher." A common English name for the whole genus is "butcherbird," referring to the shrike's habit of impaling prey too large to swallow on pointed objects. Its species name, *excubitor,* means "sentinel," describing the shrike's habit of perching for long periods on the same spot in search of prey.

While northern shrikes live a predatory lifestyle, this strikingly beautiful and tenacious passerine lacks many of the specialized adaptations of raptors, including large, powerful feet, talons and a crop. However, northern shrikes are efficient predators, hunting small birds, large insects, small mammals such as voles and mice, and amphibians. Shrikes kill prey with their beaks and kill vertebrates by repeatedly striking and biting into the neck with their beak, disarticulating cervical vertebrae, rather like falcons. But shrikes can't use their feet as weapons nor hold larger prey down with their feet while tearing them apart, like raptors.

If you take the time to study the northern shrike in Denali, you'll be rewarded with an intimate view of this somewhat rare passerine and may witness shrikes pursuing large arctic bumblebees.

MIGRATION: Most individuals breeding at high latitudes leave breeding grounds to spend the winter in southern Canada and the northern United States. But it is not unusual for northern shrikes to overwinter at high latitudes, and they are seen occasionally in interior Alaska in winter.

CONSERVATION: Many of the 30 shrike species in the world are declining or have already become extinct locally. The causes are largely unknown. While the western population of northern shrikes may be stable, the eastern subspecies has experienced a significant decline.

SPECIAL CAUTION: Northern shrikes are extremely aggressive in defense of their nest and young and may dive at the backs and heads of intruders. You should remain at least 300 feet (100 meters) away from occupied nests to avoid disturbing nesting attempts.

DENALI HABITAT: Breeds in riparian corridors and open spruce woodlands. Few known nests occur in larger shrub willows and smaller spruce.

LOCATIONS: Commonly seen near Wonder Lake, Stony Hill, Highway Pass and Sable Pass and in open woodlands and willow-filled drainages. Most often seen perched atop a spruce tree or willow, scanning the surrounding area for prey. Often heard before seen.

Common Raven
Corvus corax

How can you capture the raven's unique lifestyle and spirit in only a few words? They seem just as comfortable at more than 17,000 feet (5,000 meters) on Mt. McKinley as in the scrub deserts of Mexico. Largest of the passerines, ravens are known throughout history as both portent and prophet. More predatory than many of their fellow corvids, they kill ground squirrels and even snowshoe hares with their heavy bills. The ultimate omnivore, dumpster-diving ravens in Fairbanks have an affinity for noodles, but will eat almost anything. They delight in tearing into climbers' food caches on Mt. McKinley, and flourish in the moist beauty of Alaska's coastal southeast. They produce more than 30 vocalizations, many which have an austere beauty and strike a responsive chord in humans.

Ravens are magnificent fliers; they swagger, strut, stroll, hop and dash in and out of contact with people, exhibiting no dependence but a willingness to exploit. In fact, they treat us much like wolves and bears, always quick to pick up our scraps. They seem to delight, in writer Sherry Simpson's words, in "picking at the carcass of civilization" and are imbued with an unsettling authority. This is a bird of myth, after all; raven created mosquitoes and returned the Sun and Moon to the sky, hardly a being to trifle with.

MIGRATION: Common ravens are year-round residents in interior Alaska. They are regularly seen in Denali in winter, especially near human settlements and activity.

CONSERVATION: Because of their versatility and the availability of winter food supplies, raven populations in Alaska are stable.

DENALI HABITAT: Common ravens are found in all habitats in Denali; nests on cliffs and rock outcroppings, usually at lower elevations.

LOCATIONS: You can see ravens year-round in Denali, but they are not particularly abundant. Be sure to enjoy and study any that you do see.

BLACK-CAPPED CHICKADEE
Poecile atricapilla

Dr. Susan Sharbaugh, a researcher at the University of Alaska-Fairbanks, describes chickadees as "tiny barracudas with wings." Always searching for food, chickadees seize insects, seeds and other food with powerful bills that make even the hardiest bird-bander squirm. Sharbaugh also describes chickadees as "an excellent study in bird physiology pushed to the limit" because of the range of adaptations they possess for surviving in long subarctic winters.

While only a half-ounce (12 grams) in weight, the body of a black-capped chickadee living in this area is nearly 25 percent larger than one living at temperate latitudes. Chickadees in northern areas store more fat in the winter that provides greater insulation from the cold and more fuel for keeping warm. This species also uses nocturnal hypothermia to survive in the long subarctic night. By dropping their body temperature nearly 10°C (18° F) to a bottom limit of 30°C (86° F), their metabolic rate decreases and they conserve precious energy supplies for survival.

Chickadees cache food to ensure they have an ample supply through the winter. They have incredible memories and laboratory studies suggest that the hippocampus, the part of the brain associated with memory, increases in size as caching begins after the breeding season.

Perhaps the most amazing facet of Sharbaugh's research is the discovery of how black-capped chickadees in interior Alaska modify lipoprotein lipase (LPL), an enzyme used by many organisms to provide free fatty acids for metabolism by muscles and storage by fat. Levels of LPL in chickadees in interior Alaska are ten times higher than in birds that are preparing for migration. Chickadees maximize the capture of free fatty acids in their cells and store significant amounts of body fat in just six hours, often gaining eight to ten percent of their body mass each day.

MIGRATION: Black-capped chickadees reside throughout their range. Long-distance movements, generally by young of the year, occur irregularly every two or more years, and are considered "irruptions" rather than true migrations. Fluctuations in northern seed crops, high reproductive success (excess young), and habitat destruction seem to influence irruptions. In Alaska, black-capped chickadees usually travel in flocks consisting of breeding pairs and their young during winter.

CONSERVATION: Numbers are stable and could actually be increasing in some areas due to forest fragmentations. However, there are concerns over the health of local populations in Alaska. In the late 1990s, birdwatchers in Anchorage and the Matanuska Valley in southcentral Alaska noticed chickadees with deformed bills at their bird feeders. These birds were having difficulty feeding and often relied on suet and peanut butter as food sources. Many times, they fed on the ground, often laying on their sides to manipulate and crack seeds. Survival of these birds is probably much lower than that of normal birds because of difficulties with feeding, increases in predation when feeding on the ground, and impaired ability to preen and maintain their plumage for warmth. The cause of bill deformities is currently unknown, but researchers from the Alaska Biological Science Center are searching for answers to this mystery.

DENALI HABITAT: Mixed and deciduous woods and willow thickets. Most common where birches and alders grow, avoiding purely coniferous forests.

LOCATIONS: Savage, Sanctuary and Teklanika campground areas and the Wonder Lake area. Denali State Park and Petersville Road.

BOREAL CHICKADEE

BOREAL CHICKADEE
Poecile hudsonica

Boreal and black-capped chickadees are among the smallest of all the vertebrates in Denali that remain active in winter and do not live within the snowpack. The boreal chickadee belongs to the "brown-capped" assemblage of chickadees that also includes the gray-headed chickadee (*P. cincta*), chestnut-backed chickadee (*P. rufescens*), and Mexican chickadee (*P. sclateri*). All lack a whistled advertisement song, making it difficult to find them during the breeding season.

Boreal chickadees feed mainly on invertebrates, but also eat birch seeds. In Denali, they feed heavily on moth, butterfly and beetle larvae and spruce seeds. Like black-capped chickadees, boreals are active cachers, ensuring food throughout the winter.

According to results of Breeding Bird Surveys conducted along the Denali Park Road and Petersville Road, boreal chickadees are more common between Savage River and Teklanika River, but black-capped chickadees are more common near Toklat and along the Petersville Road. In winter, results from the Denali Christmas Bird Count suggest that boreal chickadees outnumber black-capped chickadees by five to one in areas near McKinley Park and Park Headquarters. However, on the Trapper Creek–Talkeetna Christmas Bird Count, black-capped chickadees outnumber boreal chickadees by nearly 22 to 1.

Many sightings of gray-headed chickadees have been reported in Denali, however, no specimen, photographic record, or well-described, multi-observer sight records exist. Encounters of gray-headed chickadees in Denali should be well-documented (with photographs, if possible) and reported to a park ranger or park staff.

MIGRATION: Boreal chickadees are generally considered non-migratory, but with a tendency towards irruption. Conifer forests of Alaska and Canada provide primary year-round range, and the northern limit of the species in Alaska coincides with white spruce distribution. Although boreal chickadees are rarely found south of Canada, extreme winter records exist from Virginia, Iowa, Illinois and Indiana.

CONSERVATION: Although there is a limited amount of reliable information available, this species appears to be stable. It is not confined to mature forests, although it seems to prefer them.

DENALI HABITAT: Found year-round in white spruce forests.

LOCATIONS: Park Headquarters, Savage, Sanctuary, Teklanika, and Igloo Campgrounds, and in the Wonder Lake area; forests along Parks Highway and Petersville Road.

AMERICAN DIPPER
Cinclus mexicanus

The American dipper is North America's only truly submersible songbird. The name fits this bird well as it dips up and down nearly 40 times per minute while perched. All members of the the dipper family live beside swift, unpolluted rocky streams, feeding mostly on aquatic insect larvae, but also on other invertebrates, fish eggs, small fish and flying insects. They forage in the water and are totally dependent on the productivity of rivers and streams for their well-being.

John Muir, among others, admired the dipper's swimming skills in deep, swift water where people cannot stand upright. He called them "the hummingbirds of blooming waters, loving rocky ripple-slopes and sheets of foam." Tiny flaps seal off their nostrils, letting dippers hunt under water, while a second, transparent set of eyelids serve as goggles. Dippers feed in turbulent waters even at temperatures well below 0° C. To survive in harsh subarctic ecosystems, these little birds have low metabolic rates, extra-oxygen-carrying capacity in their blood, and a thick coat of feathers.

The distribution and abundance of dippers is not well-known in Denali. A winter sighting of a dipper is always a memorable experience. This species is seen regularly on the Trapper Creek--Talkeetna Christmas Bird Count. MIGRATION: There are no reports of long-distance migrations for this species. Most dippers stay in interior Alaska during the winter, searching out open stretches of water for foraging. Altitudinal movements in spring and fall enable dippers to avoid frozen habitat in winter and disperse widely during breeding.

CONSERVATION: Dippers serve as good indicators of stream health and water quality. Because of this, some state agencies outside of Alaska have designated it a species of concern. Dipper populations may be vulnerable in the United States due to environmental contaminants.

DENALI HABITAT: Swift, unpolluted, rocky streams.

LOCATIONS: In winter and early spring, dippers are often seen along the Savage River near Savage River bridge; in summer look for dippers along Igloo Creek, Moose Creek, and many of the other clearwater streams in Denali National Park, as well as Byers Creek, Troublesome Creek, Trapper Creek and similar streams in and around Denali State Park.

Arctic Warbler
Phylloscopus borealis

The arctic warbler is an Old World passerine that originated in Siberia and established itself in Alaska following the last great ice age. A late spring migrant, arctic warblers are not seen consistently until mid-June when they become common along Igloo Creek and elsewhere. Their raspy, loud, unwarblerlike calls are unmistakable, and you'll hear them singing tirelessly throughout the long subarctic day. Adolph Murie found the first two nests of this species recorded in North America among the willows along Igloo Creek in 1955. One nest was in the opening of a rodent tunnel and the other on moss-covered ground. Both nests were dome-shaped, built from fine grass and caribou hair, roofed over with loosely piled moss, and entered from one side.

MIGRATION: Fall migration begins by mid-August and the entire Alaskan population returns to eastern Asia before flying south with the Siberian population to the wintering grounds in southeastern China, Indonesia, the Philippines and Borneo.

CONSERVATION: Basic breeding biology of this species in not well described anywhere in its range. Fragmentation and destruction of wintering and migratory stopover habitat could influence survival of this species.

DENALI HABITAT: Tendency toward medium-height willow thickets in riparian areas as well as low to tall willows near treeline, and in open white spruce woodlands.

LOCATIONS: Igloo Canyon is one of the best places to see arctic warblers in Denali. They may also be found in the upper Petersville Road area. Listen and look for them in willow thickets in riparian areas throughout the area, but make sure to keep an eye out for grizzlies as well!

Northern Wheatear
Oenanthe oenanthe

Scan the alpine tundra with your binoculars to find these long-legged passerines perched on rocks, standing erect with their tails pumping up and down, waiting patiently for the next insect to come into range. With little apparent effort, a northern wheatear bursts into the air, snaps up its target, and returns to its perch to wait for the next vulnerable insect.

Family groups are common sights in Denali in mid- to late July. Juveniles in these groups are often very vocal, their raspy voices carrying far across these open landscapes. The northern wheatear is an elegant Old World bird that lives in alpine habitats in Alaska and Canada in summer and steppe and savanna habitat in sub-Sahara Africa in winter. Wheatears depart Denali by mid-August, leaving behind quiet and seemingly barren tundra.

MIGRATION: The exact migration routes of northern wheatears between Alaska and sub-Sahara Africa are not documented. Routes probably exist across Asia and the Middle East into the wintering areas in sub-Sahara Africa.

CONSERVATION: Population status of northern wheatears is not well-documented in Alaska and Yukon. This species is not observed on many Breeding Bird Surveys and is not adequately covered by other ongoing bird surveys in Alaska. Identification and conservation of breeding, wintering, and migratory stop-over habitat for this species is imperative for its long-term survival.

SPECIAL CAUTION: Like many ground-nesting birds, northern wheatears are very sensitive to disturbance and will readily desert their nests. Please don't approach the nest of any ground nesting species of birds in Denali

DENALI HABITAT: Open, alpine areas.

LOCATIONS: Primrose Ridge, Sable Pass, Upper Tattler Creek, Polychrome, Stony Creek, and Eielson Visitor Center area in Denali National Park, Kesugi Ridge in Denali State Park, and in the Peters Hills.

GREY-CHEEKED THRUSH
Catharus minimus

Shy and elusive, the haunting song of the grey-cheeked thrush drifts across the boreal landscape during the long subarctic dawn. A brief summer visitor to its boreal breeding areas, the grey-cheeked thrush spends most of its life among the native broad-leaf forests of Central and South America. Grey-cheeked thrushes have proportionately longer legs than many passerines and are well adapted for nesting and foraging near and on the floors of boreal and tropical forests. They are the most northern breeding of all the North American *Catharus* thrushes.

MIGRATION: The grey-cheeked thrush is the champion migrant of all

Cathurus thrushes. The average distance between their wintering and breeding grounds is about 3,800 miles (6,200 kilometers). Migrating mostly at night, birds from Alaska and eastern Siberia migrate far to the east before turning southward. In autumn, some individuals make a non-stop flight from northeastern North America to northern South America. In spring, many northbound thrushes stopover in the narrow bands of woodlands and wooded barrier islands of the Gulf of Mexico to rest, feed and wait out storms. These productive woodlands are extremely important for the long-term viability of all *Cathurus* thrushes. The wintering grounds include southern Mexico, the West Indies, Peru, Brazil and British Guyana.

CONSERVATION: The persistence of migrant populations of birds depends on their ability to find favorable conditions throughout their annual cycle. The National Audubon Society lists the grey-cheeked thrush on its Alaska WatchList because of concerns over its population status and threats to wintering habitat, particularly destruction of broad-leaf tropical forests. It is also listed as a species of conservation priority by Boreal Partners in Flight and a species of special concern by the Alaska Department of Fish and Game.

DENALI HABITAT: Grey-cheeked thrushes are found in a variety of habitats, including willow and alder thickets in lowland, upland and subalpine areas; upland and riparian deciduous woodlands; coniferous forests and woodlands.

LOCATIONS: Teklanika Campground, Cathedral Mountain, Sable and Polychrome Passes, Wonder Lake area, Troublesome and Byers Creeks, Petersville Road.

SWAINSON'S THRUSH
Catharus ustulatus

The ethereal, upward-spiraling song of the Swainson's thrush is one of the top notes of Denali's twilight thrush serenade. The voices of the five species of cryptically colored thrushes in the genus *Catharus* are among the finest in North America. Our ears cannot register the complexity of this vocalization unless it is recorded and played back at one-quarter speed. Only then can we appreciate the intricacies of the songs. If you spend time in a campground in the Denali area, you'll be rewarded with the enchanting serenade of this boreal thrush.

MIGRATION: The majority of Swainson's thrushes are from southern Mexico to Peru, Brazil and Argentina. A few individuals may winter in the West Indies.

CONSERVATION: Swainson's thrushes may require intact forests, unlike many other migrants, and might be more susceptible to rainforest destruction than other species.

DENALI HABITAT: Spruce-poplar forests and spruce woodlands.

LOCATIONS: From the park entrance to around mile 6 on Denali Park Road; Teklanika Campground; Wonder Lake; woodlands in area of Denali State Park; singing under cabin windows at Byers Lake!

VARIED THRUSH
Ixoreus naevius

An early spring migrant in interior Alaska, the extra-terrestrial song of the varied thrush brings a smile to many Alaskans as they emerge from winter. Described as a referee's whistle, alarm clock, kazoo, British policeman's whistle, eerie bell-like call, or metallic whistle, the song of the varied thrush conjures visions of spaceships to more than one Alaskan birder. A common species in the Pacific Northwest, where they are known as "rain robins," they inhabit coniferous forests in Denali. An evening or early morning visit to a spruce forest will leave you with mixed emotions and probably with a stiff neck; while you'll enjoy the calls surrounding you in the forest, you'll strain to get a quick glimpse of this forest ventriloquist.

MIGRATION: Varied thrushes from Alaska probably winter throughout the Pacific Northwest, including southeast Alaska.

DENALI HABITAT: Dense spruce forest with lush understory.

CONSERVATION: Varied thrushes spend most of their lives in coniferous forests. The logging of old-growth forests is probably the greatest conservation concern for this species.

LOCATIONS: Spruce forests, especially in eastern portion of Denali National Park, Kantishna area, Byers Lake and Parks Highway south to Trapper Creek.

Bohemian Waxwing
Bombycilla garrulus

Small flocks of Bohemian waxwings are seen and heard in Denali in summer as they sally out from the treetops in pursuit of insects. The name "Bohemian" reflects their rather unconventional and seemingly carefree lifestyle as sociable nomads in winter, when they gather in large flocks in search of berries. The high, thin, trilling call notes, sung both in flight and from treetops, is diagnostic. Nesting in loose colonies, the young continue to associate with their parents after fledging and may remain with them through the first fall migration and winter.

MIGRATION: Movements of Bohemian waxwings are highly variable. While they migrate as far as California, Texas and the central Atlantic coast, they are commonly seen throughout the winter in Fairbanks, where they survive by feeding on freeze-dried ornamental chokecherries. This species is recorded consistently and in good numbers on recent Anchorage and Fairbanks Christmas Bird Counts, but has not been recorded on either the Denali or Talkeetna Christmas Bird Count.

CONSERVATION: Assessing the conservation status of this species is difficult because its wandering lifestyle makes it nearly impossible to obtain an accurate census.

DENALI HABITAT: Open coniferous forests, muskegs and mixed coniferous-deciduous woodlands.

LOCATIONS: Triple Lakes, Denali Park Headquarters area to mile 6 on Denali Park Road, Wonder Lake area, and Denali State Park.

Blackpoll Warbler
Dendroica striata

The high-pitched, insect-like, soft "song" of the blackpoll warbler is an unmistakable sound in Denali's boreal forests, but is easily missed amidst other songsters and the buzz of mosquitoes. These insectivores breed across the northern coniferous forests of North America. Despite their wide range and well-known migratory lifestyle, most aspects of this species have not been well studied.

Blackpoll warblers are celebrities in the migration world. Their annual journeys between North America and South America are among the longest in the bird world. To successfully complete these journeys, blackpolls must obtain and use energy efficiently. Gathering in flocks on pre-migratory staging areas, blackpolls quickly pack on fat. Scientist James Baird describes this rapid pre-migratory fattening (or hyperphagia) as "gluttony with a purpose." Once laden with fat, they're very fuel efficient. According to researchers Tim and Janet Williams, "if blackpoll warblers were burning gasoline instead of reserves of body fat, they could boast of getting 720,000 miles to the gallon (30,500 kilometers to the liter)."

MIGRATION: Dr. Kenneth Able calls the migratory odyssey of blackpoll warblers one of the "greatest tests of endurance engaged in by any animal." The actual migratory routes of blackpoll warblers from Alaska are not known, but we know that they migrate between here and their wintering areas in South America. In autumn, they probably journey southeast through Canada and meet up with other flocks of pre-migratory blackpolls warblers somewhere in the northeastern portion of North America. They then head out over the western Atlantic on an over-water journey south to their wintering areas.

CONSERVATION: Blackpoll warblers are listed as a priority species for conservation by the Boreal Partners in Flight working group due to concerns over their population trends and loss of wintering habitat. This species is considered "highly vulnerable" to tropical forest deforestation and results from the North American Breeding Bird Survey suggest that populations are declining across North America. Significant numbers are killed at towers, lighthouses, tall buildings and other tall structures during migration.

DENALI HABITAT: Taiga forest to timberline, alder and willow thickets, riparian areas at lower elevations.

LOCATIONS: Forested areas along the Denali Park Road from the entrance area to mile 6, from the Sanctuary River to Igloo Creek, Toklat area, and Moose Creek area in Kantishna. Along the Parks Highway around Montana Creek, Trapper Creek to the Alaska Veterans Memorial and Byers Lake and Carlo Creek.

Northern Waterthrush
Seiurus noveboracensis

"Loud and low" might be the best way to describe northern waterthrushes. Found amongst tangles of thick vegetation and clouds of mosquitoes, their loud voices are often the only indication of their presence. Although it is a warbler and not a thrush, the species is aptly named–the waterthrush lives most of its life near water and acts more like a ground-dwelling thrush than an arboreal warbler. Finding it often results in wet feet, a small price to pay to catch a glimpse of this beautiful warbler.

MIGRATION: Northern waterthrushes are long-distance migrants. They winter in Mexico, Caribbean, Central America and northern South America.

CONSERVATION: A classic study completed by P. Schwartz in Caracas, Venezuela, in the 1960s showed that wintering northern waterthrushes defended their foraging areas against intruders and had strong fidelity to wintering territories. As John Terborgh points out in his book *Where Have All the Birds Gone*, these findings are important for understanding the habits and habitat needs of long-distance migrants. If these birds return to the same area year after year, it is imperative that we conserve habitat in these areas for their long-term survival. According to results from the Breeding Bird Survey, northern waterthrush populations in North America are relatively stable. However, in winter, this species inhabits rapidly disappearing mangrove forests in Central and South America. Also, this species depends on migratory stop-over habitat for refueling during its long journeys.

DENALI HABITAT: Forested wetlands, bogs, swamps and riparian corridors.

LOCATIONS: Horseshoe Lake, brushy edges of tundra ponds west of Eielson Visitor Center to Wonder Lake, "Big Timber" area along McKinley Bar Trail, edges of Moose Creek in Kantishna Hills; Denali State Park and Petersville Road/Trapper Creek in appropriate habitat.

WILSON'S WARBLER
Wilsonia pusilla

These bright bundles of animation go about their daily chores of securing food with zest and excitement. Wilson's warblers are one of the "fly-catching" warblers. They dart after flying insects and capture them with an audible snap of their bill. Wilson's warblers are one of the most abundant warblers occurring on the north side of the Alaska Range in Denali. They are the most commonly captured species at the Denali Institute's fall migration station near Kantishna. The males return to Denali in mid-May, with the females arriving up to ten days later. They are widespread across North America, but are not well studied.

MIGRATION: Wilson's warblers leave Alaska from mid- to late August. They winter from northern Mexico and southern Texas south to Costa Rica and western Panama.

CONSERVATION: Wilson's warblers are one of the most common nearctic-neotropical migrants in the western United States. According to the results of the Breeding Bird Survey, Wilson's warbler numbers have declined continent-wide over the last two decades, but in Alaska their population appears stable. Survival of all long-distance migrants depends on many factors, including food availability and habitat along autumn and spring migration routes. Wilson's warblers are long-distance migrants and they must feed and rest during their journeys. Many of these stopover areas are located in riparian areas where native vegetation is being destroyed. While this species winters in a variety of habitats, it is still vulnerable to destruction of tropical forests.

DENALI HABITAT: Alder, willow and dwarf birch in moist clearings, especially along streams, ponds and bogs; and at various elevations in the mountains in shrubs of valley bottoms, mountainsides and alpine meadows. Avoids interior of dense forests.

LOCATIONS: Savage River, Igloo Creek, Tattler Creek, Wonder Lake area, Curry and Kesugi Ridges, Peters Hills.

DAS 2000

Fox Sparrow

Passerella iliaca

The fox sparrow's song, which varies from one subspecies to another, is perhaps the most beautiful of any of the sparrows. Its rich song, described as dreamy, is commonly heard in Denali from late May throughout June. Recent investigation into the systematics of this bird will likely result in a split into three or four separate species. Meanwhile, birders can contrast the fox sparrow of Denali (subspecies *zaboria*) with the quite dissimilar *sinuosa* of Upper Cook Inlet and the Kenai Peninsula. They could even document possible occurrences of non-*zaboria* forms in the Denali area. Known as "roto-tiller" birds to some local birders, these hardy sparrows often forage on the ground, kicking up leaf letter and soil with their large feet as they search for prey.

MIGRATION: Most of *zaboria* winter east of the Great Plains, from eastern Kansas to Texas, Georgia, Louisiana, Mississippi and Alabama; rarely west to Washington, California and Arizona.

CONSERVATION STATUS: Like many species of birds that winter in North America, conservation of this species relies on preservation of wintering habitat. This includes preventing habitat fragmentation and alteration, and preventing unwise use of chemicals in our environment.

DENALI HABITAT: Thickets to the upper limits of taller brush.

LOCATIONS: Denali Park Road corridor; Sable Pass; western half of the Wonder Lake road especially good; fairly common south of Denali State Park to Trapper Creek and on the Petersville Road.

LINCOLN'S SPARROW
Melospiza lincolnii

To find this bird in Denali, you must learn its extraordinary song, which some find wren-like. Lincoln's sparrow has a well-deserved reputation as a skulker, and this, along with a marked affinity for wet, brushy, buggy habitat that many humans find objectionable, makes a search for this species always memorable. The best place to listen and see them near Denali is along the Petersville Road, near Talkeetna, where they are one of the most abundant species recorded on the Breeding Bird Survey. In any case, be sure to bring plenty of insect repellent along on your search for this little songster.

MIGRATION: Lincoln's sparrows breed in sub-arctic or alpine areas from northern Mexico and California, and throughout the boreal forest regions of Alaska and Canada. No banded Lincoln's sparrow has ever been recovered between breeding and wintering grounds. Lincoln's sparrows winter along the west coast of the U.S., and across the southwestern and southcentral U.S., throughout Mexico, as far south as Costa Rica.

CONSERVATION: Lincoln's sparrows respond quickly to changes in ground cover and food supplies. Despite a demonstrated vulnerability to some herbicides, Lincoln's sparrows are numerous and widespread. Only in Quebec and the northern spruce hardwood forests has any recent decline been documented. The conservation of this species, as for many species, depends on habitat preservation on both wintering and breeding grounds.

DENALI HABITAT: Boggy areas with sedges or especially willows.

LOCATIONS: Tundra ponds west of Eielson Visitor Center on the way to Wonder Lake and Kantishna; Wonder Lake; Denali State Park and Petersville Road in appropriate habitat.

LAPLAND LONGSPUR

Calcarius lapponicus

Strikingly handsome, Lapland longspurs are one of the most common tundra inhabitants in Denali. Easily recognized by appearance and flight song, males sing a sparkling jumble of notes during the breeding season, including a musical "tee-lee-oo" and in flight, a dry rattle mixed with "tew" notes.

Large flocks of longspurs arrive in central Alaska in May. Generally, the males migrate earlier than females and arrive on breeding grounds before them. Nesting success can be influenced by spring weather conditions and is often low during late, wet springs.

Lapland longspurs are circumpolar breeders. They are abundant and widespread at high latitudes in North America, Greenland, Europe and Asia. In Alaska, longspurs are most abundant in the western and northern regions of the state. The rarer and more sought after Smith's longspur is rarely seen in Denali, but is regularly observed along the nearby Denali Highway.

MIGRATION: Longspurs migrate in flocks that often number into the hundreds and sometimes thousands. In central Alaska, fall migration occurs from mid-August to mid-September. This species winters primarily in the western United States, especially the Great Plains region and southern Canada.

CONSERVATION: While this species is abundant and widespread, there is growing concern for the stability of its wintering habitat. This concern is highest in the grassland ecosystems of North America where exotic vegetation is rapidly replacing native vegetation.

DENALI HABITAT: Open habitats including tussock tundra.

LOCATIONS: Primrose Ridge; Highway Pass to Thorofare Pass and similar habitats in subalpine and alpine areas in Denali National Park. On Kesugi and Curry ridges and Peters Hill in Denali State Park.

White-winged Crossbill

Loxia leucoptera

The bright plumage of this species offers relief to the eyes in the winter landscape of Denali. White-winged crossbills are nomads of the northern forests. Often seen in large, noisy flocks, these large and conspicuous birds make their way across northern forests in search of conifer seeds.

MIGRATION: White-winged crossbills move across North America from Alaska to Newfoundland in search of conifer seeds. Movements can occur anytime, but the magnitude of their movements is determined by the distribution and availability of conifer seeds.

CONSERVATION: Like other birds that rely on highly variable food sources, white-winged crossbills are difficult to study. They are particularly dependent upon coniferous seeds and, consequently, upon the spruce forests of interior Alaska. Anything that influences the production of conifer seeds affects crossbill population dynamics. Increases in logging, invasions by insects, fire and climate change could impact the availability of conifer seeds for this species.

DENALI HABITAT: Seed-producing coniferous forests.

LOCATIONS: Along the Denali Park Road from the entrance to mile 6; forests along the Teklanika and Toklat Rivers and in the Wonder Lake area. Forests in Denali State Park.

COMMON REDPOLL
Carduelis flammea

Studies suggest that redpolls can tolerate colder temperatures than any other small passerine. Like chickadees, common redpolls depend on a series of unique adaptations to survive in these harsh environments. Their plumage weight in winter is nearly twice that of summer and they often erect their feathers in winter to retain heat. Redpolls store seeds in a pouch in their esophagus. This unique storage system allows redpolls to take on large amounts of high-calorie foods before nightfall and digest these seeds after they have gone to roost. Like chickadees, redpolls seek out sheltered places for roosts during dark hours and during particularly inclement weather.

Gregarious year-round, they are only one of a few songbirds that are not territorial during the breeding season. In summer, they are easily overlooked until their calls are learned; the buzzy calls of redpolls commonly heard as they fly high overhead give a good indication of how common this species is in Denali. Their numbers in summer and winter, however, vary greatly. For instance, the number of redpolls recorded on the Denali Christmas Bird Count from 1992 to 1999 ranged from one to 360 individuals. Great variation in redpoll numbers is also recorded on the Fairbanks Christmas Bird Count where the number of individuals observed per year ranged from 36 to 2,238.

MIGRATION: Common redpolls are largely nomadic outside the breeding season. They display irregular migratory movements by streaming south from northern areas every few years during the winter months. Scientists

suggest that redpoll populations shift in accordance with food supplies, mainly seeds and catkins of birch, alder, willow, and spruce. Large numbers of common redpolls head south when birch catkins are low in abundance. In these years, many redpolls frequent feeders throughout the northern United States. In the Fairbanks area, huge flocks of redpolls, often numbering in the hundreds, roam through birch forests in search of food during early winter. Carpets of shredded birch catkins blanketing the snow-covered forest floor are evidence of the feeding frenzies of these huge flocks.
Despite the availability of feeders in Fairbanks, most redpolls don't start frequenting feeders until after early January.

CONSERVATION: Common redpoll populations are thought to be stable, however, it is difficult to determine the status of these populations due to their lack of fidelity to breeding and winter areas, and their irruptive behavior. Changes in distribution and productivity of northern forest may influence food supplies for this species.

DENALI HABITAT: Brush at all elevations; sometimes spruce.

LOCATIONS: Can be found where the Denali Park Road, Parks Highway, and Petersville Road intersect with brushy willows or alders.